WORLD RELIGIONS

ISLAM

BY LUCIA RAATMA

Content Adviser:
Mohamed Elsanousi, Director,
Communications and Community Outreach,
Islamic Society of North America

Reading Adviser:
Alexa L. Sandmann, Ed.D., Professor of Literacy,
College and Graduate School of Education,
Health, and Human Services, Kent State University

475
Clifton Park, New York

Compass Point Books
151 Good Counsel Drive
P.O. Box 669
Mankato, MN 56002-0669

 This book was manufactured with paper containing
at least 10 percent post-consumer waste.

Photographs ©: AP Images: Hassan Ammar 23; Art Resource, N.Y.: Erich
Lessing 24; The Bridgeman Art Library: Bibliotheque Nationale, Paris, France
33; Corbis: dpa/Tim Brakemeier 36–37; Getty Images: AFP/Arif Ali 39, AFP/
Osservatore Romano 42–43, Bill Pugliano 41, Muhannad Fala'ah 4–5, 7, The
Bridgeman Art Library 30; iStockphoto: Damir Cudic 11, DistinctiveImages
cover, Duncan Walker 32, Frank Leung 31, Karen Moller 16–17, Robert Churchill
19, Vladimir Melnik 22; Shutterstock: ayazad 26–27, Catherine Jones (design
element) cover (top and bottom), back cover (top), 1, 45, sidebars throughout,
Juriah Mosin 21, maga (background texture) 4, 9, 15, 23, 36, 46, 47, Sinan
Isakovic 15, Sufi 25; Wikimedia: Evgenia Kononova 12, Nazli 9.

Editor: Brenda Haugen
Designers: Ashlee Suker and Bobbie Nuytten
Media Researcher: Svetlana Zhurkin
Library Consultant: Kathleen Baxter
Cartographer: XNR Productions, Inc.
Art Director: LuAnn Ascheman-Adams
Creative Director: Joe Ewest
Editorial Director: Nick Healy
Managing Editor: Catherine Neitge

Library of Congress Cataloging-in-Publication Data
Raatma, Lucia.
  Islam / by Lucia Raatma.
     p. cm.—(World religions)
  Includes index.
  ISBN 978-0-7565-4239-9 (library binding)
  1. Islam—Juvenile literature. 2. Islam—History—Juvenile
literature. I. Title. II. Series.
  BP161.3.R32 2010
  297—dc22   5842   2009015812

Visit Compass Point Books on the Internet at *www.compasspointbooks.com*
or e-mail your request to *custserv@compasspointbooks.com*

Table of Contents

Chapter One

ON THE ROAD
TO MECCA

Muslims from all over the world heed the call
to make a pilgrimage to Mecca, known as a *hajj*.
Each year during Dhu al-Hijja, the last month
of the Islamic year, they come by
plane, by boat, and on foot,
usually arriving at
Jeddah, a port in Saudi
Arabia that is about
4.5 miles

Muslims Around the World

The followers of Islam, called Muslims, live in many parts of the world. The largest groups are in Saudi Arabia, Iran, Iraq, and other countries in the Middle East, as well as in Pakistan and Afghanistan. But many African, Asian, and European countries are home to Muslims as well. About 6 million Muslims live in the United States, and more than 500,000 live in Canada.

(72 kilometers) from the sacred city of Mecca. As they get closer to the city, they pause to shower and change clothes. They wear white cotton clothing for their appearance before Allah, the Muslim name for God.

As the crowd enters Mecca, they begin to chant in Arabic. The English translation begins: "Here I am, oh God, at your command." The chanting of thousands of people echoes all around.

The main reason for the hajj is to remember the prophet Ibrahim's willingness to sacrifice his first-born son, Ismail, at Allah's command and the path to the altar where Satan tried three times to talk Ibrahim out of the sacrifice. Muslims believe that in the end, Allah stopped Ibrahim,

Male pilgrims on the hajj wear two white sheets wrapped around their bodies. Dressing this way reminds them of the holiness of their journey and also shows that they are united and equal, regardless of their wealth or class.

satisfied that he was willing to sacrifice his son out of obedience to Allah. Christians, Jews, and Baha'is also consider Abraham (Ibrahim) one of their religious leaders.

By the first night of the hajj, millions of people have gathered. They camp in tents in the village of Mina, close to Mecca. The tents are white and form huge tent cities. The pilgrims spend time reading and praying.

The next day, the pilgrims travel to the Plain of Arafat. There they sit near the Mount of Mercy, asking Allah for forgiveness for all their sins. After a full day of prayer, they leave at sunset and spend time collecting small stones. They will need those the next day.

In the morning, they awake before sunrise. As the light fills the sky, they begin throwing the stones at pillars that represent the temptations of Satan.

During the hajj, pilgrims sacrifice animals, often sheep or goats, and offer the meat to people who are poor. This sacrifice is celebrated as Eid al-Adha, a major holiday in Islam, the Muslim religion.

Finally the millions of pilgrims return to Mecca. There they circle the Kaaba, one of Islam's holiest sites, and visit Safa and Marwa, two small hills nearby. It is here where Ismail's mother, Hagar, is said to have searched for water for her son when he was a baby. The pilgrims remember the work that Ibrahim put

Pilgrims throw stones at each of three pillars in Mina, Saudi Arabia. This ceremony symbolizes their belief that people should cast away the evil of Satan repeatedly and resolve not to listen to him ever again.

into rebuilding the Kaaba. Then they drink from a sacred spring called Zamzam.

The hajj is officially over, but many pilgrims remain in the region. They visit the city of Medina and they honor the burial site of Muhammad, who founded the religion of Islam in 622. Today Islam is the faith of more than a billion people around the world.

Muslims are required to make the pilgrimage to Mecca at least once if they can afford it and are physically able. It is a time of remembrance and prayer. It also is a time to learn about the history of their religion and to strengthen their faith.

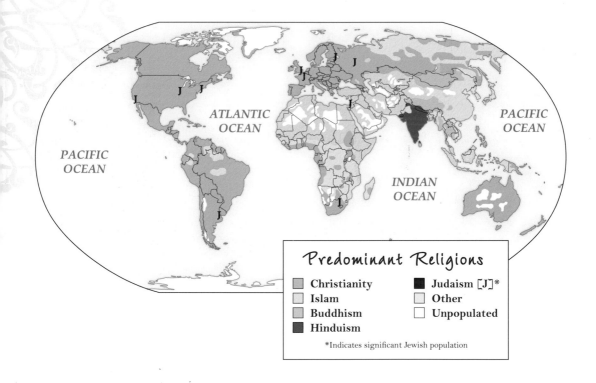

Predominant Religions

- Christianity
- Islam
- Buddhism
- Hinduism
- Judaism [J]*
- Other
- Unpopulated

*Indicates significant Jewish population

Chapter Two

FOUNDER AND BELIEFS

When he was about 40 years old, Muhammad often went to the Cave of Hira on Jabal al-Nour ("Mountain of Light") to meditate. The Cave of Hira is outside Mecca in what today is the nation of Saudi Arabia. Muhammad's visits to the cave were in 610, about 1,400 years ago.

The Cave of Hira is only about 11.5 feet (3.5 meters) long and a little over 5 feet (1.5 m) wide.

Muslims believe that as Muhammad was meditating one day, he heard a voice. It was the voice of the angel Jibrail. The angel said to him, "Proclaim!" Muhammad asked what he should proclaim. "Proclaim," the angel commanded again, and then: "Proclaim in the name of your Lord who created! Created man from a clot of blood. Proclaim: Your Lord is the most generous, who teaches by the pen; teaches man what he knew not." At first Muhammad could not recite the words, but then he went on to say the words that are now the verses in the 96th chapter of the Qur'an, the holy book of the Islam faith.

For the next 23 years, Muhammad continued to receive revelations from Jibrail. It is said that he memorized these words, and his companions wrote them

The Qur'an is Islam's most sacred text.

down, thus creating the Qur'an. Some people in Mecca welcomed his message, but others did not like what Muhammad was preaching. In 622, when he realized his life was in danger, Muhammad and some of his followers left Mecca and moved to Medina. This move was known as the *hijrah*, which means "the flight." It's considered to be the starting time for Islam.

Islam teaches that there is only one god, whose name in Arabic is Allah. The word *Islam* comes from the Arabic word *aslama*, which means "to surrender or submit." A person who follows Islam is a Muslim, a term that means "one who submits to God." Muslims show

A painting showing an angel stopping Ibrahim from sacrificing his son is in the Haft Tanan museum in Shiraz, Iran.

their devotion to Allah by worshipping him, rejecting religions with many gods, and following Allah's commandments.

Muslims believe that Muhammad was Allah's final prophet. Prophets are people whom God has chosen as messengers. According to the Qur'an, prophets who came before Muhammad included Ibrahim, Noah, Moses, and Jesus. When Muhammad was visited by Jibrail, Christianity and Judaism were already established religions. Muslims believe that Muhammad was sent to make clear the messages of Allah.

The people of Islam follow the Six Articles of Faith. These include beliefs in Allah, his teachings, his angels, his prophets, and a final judgment day. For Muslims there is but one God, and he created the universe. The teachings of Allah are found in the Qur'an. Muslims believe that Allah uses angels to deal with humans. They believe each person has two angels—one who

Six Articles of Faith

According to the Six Articles of Faith, to be a Muslim, one must believe in:

1. One God

2. The angels of God

3. The books of God, especially the Qur'an

4. The prophets of God, especially Muhammad

5. The Day of Judgment

6. The supremacy of God's will

records good deeds and another who records bad deeds. They also believe there will be judgment by Allah at the end of a person's life. Someone who follows Allah and Muhammad will go to Paradise. Those who don't will go to Hell.

There are separate groups within Islam, including the Sunni, Shi'a, and Sufi. The Sunni and the Shi'a have conflicting beliefs about the first leaders of their religion. The Sufis embrace a spiritual and personal version of Islam.

The Sunni are the largest group within Islam,

The Five Pillars

The Shadahah	belief that there is no God except Allah and the prophet Muhammad is Allah's messenger
Salah	word for prayer; Muslims are supposed to pray five times a day, facing the Kaaba, a holy building in Mecca
Zakah	giving of money, which is a requirement of Islam; some of the money helps those in need, and some is used to spread the word of Islam
Sawm	practice of fasting during the Islamic holy month of Ramadan; Muslims are not allowed to drink or eat anything during the day for this month (young children and people with health problems don't have to follow this practice as closely)
The Hajj	pilgrimage, or journey, to the city of Mecca; every Muslim who can make the trip is supposed to do so, at least once

making up about 85 percent of Muslims, and they follow the Five Pillars of Islam. The Shi'a follow similar guidelines, but with three additional ideals: resisting evil, living a virtuous life, and obeying *jihad*. Jihad is the religious duty of Muslims to try to live in the way of Allah. Over the years, jihad has taken on military meanings and is sometimes associated with holy wars. In some cases, jihad has been associated with acts of violence and terror. But to most Muslims, it is a positive and peaceful way of living according to their beliefs.

Chapter Three

SACRED TEXT AND WORSHIP

"Allahu Akbar, Allahu Akbar!" Five times a day these Arabic words are called out in Muslim communities. A person called a *muezzin* stands in a minaret, the tallest point on a mosque, and calls everyone to prayer. In English the words mean "God is

Prayer is an important part of the Islamic faith. Most Muslims pray several times a day in mosques or in their homes.

15

most great." This chant reminds everyone it is time to stop and pray to Allah.

Muslims take off their shoes before entering a mosque, their place of worship. There are no chairs or benches in a mosque, and everyone kneels on mats to pray.

Generally men and women pray separately. For example, men and women may sit on opposite sides

Muslim men pray in a mosque in Cairo, Egypt.

Muslims at Prayer

Muslims must prepare themselves before they begin to pray. First they wash in a special way, called *wudu*. They wash their faces, and then their hands and forearms. Next they wipe their heads and wash their feet. Finally they stand, bow, kneel, and bend forward, touching the ground with their foreheads. Then Muslims are ready to pray.

of an aisle, or men may sit in front of the women. Some say the separation is traditional, while others say it helps to avoid distraction during worship.

For Muslims Friday is an important day. At noon each Friday, they attend worship and usually not in their local mosque, but in a larger one. An *imam* or other religious leader gives a *khutbah*, which is like a sermon. These talks are usually about religious matters, but they may also address community issues or social problems. Often businesses close on Friday afternoons so everyone can attend worship services.

Muslims are careful about their diets. They place great importance on healthy eating. They eat fruits and vegetables, and they avoid alcohol. Muslims do not eat any food that comes from pigs, such as bacon, because this meat is considered unclean. Muslims eat meat, but

The Qur'an

The Qur'an is Islam's holy book. It's written in Arabic, the official language of Islam. The word Qur'an means "recitation." Within the Qur'an are 114 chapters, called surahs, and they have thousands of verses. Muslims believe that the Qur'an is the word of Allah, and they turn to this book to help them live the way Allah wants them to. The Qur'an is treated with great respect. Some Muslims cover their copies with cloth to keep them clean. Sometimes Muslims place the Qur'an on a wooden stand to read it. Some keep the Qur'an on a high shelf and never place another book above it.

Muslims' diets include a variety of fruits and vegetables, such as those found at a morning market in Kota Bharu, Malaysia.

only if it comes from animals that have been slaughtered according to Islamic rules. These rules include letting all the blood out and not saying the name of any deity other than Allah during the slaughter. Such approved food is called *halal.* Many Muslims enjoy coffee and mint tea, pastries made with honey, and a variety of spices, such as cumin and cardamom.

Muslims follow certain rules of etiquette, which are ways to respectfully treat one another. For instance, they greet one another with the phrase "Salamu alaykum," which means "Peace be unto you." Before eating, they say "bismillah," which means "in the name of Allah."

The Islamic calendar is based on the cycles of the moon. There are 12 months in each calendar year, but they begin and end with each new moon. That means there are about 354 days in an Islamic year, which is about 11 days fewer than the calendar that much of the world follows.

Muslims cherish their families and other relation-

Ramadan

The observance of Ramadan takes places in the ninth month of the Islamic calendar. It honors the month in which the Qur'an is said to have been revealed to Muhammad. During this month, most Muslims fast from sunrise to sunset. They do this to purify themselves and to know what it is like to be hungry. Before sunrise, they are allowed a small meal, called *sahur*. And after sunset they eat a meal called *iftar*.

During Ramadan many Muslims try to read the entire Qur'an. They pray and think about God. They also give money and food to those who are needy or hungry.

At the end of Ramadan, Muslims celebrate the joyous festival of Eid al-Fitr. They wear new clothes, share food, have carnivals, and dance.

ships. A father is considered the head of a household, and family members rely on him to support them. In some Islamic countries, few women have jobs outside the home. Usually women are expected to care for the family.

In some countries, Muslim men are allowed to have more than one wife, but a woman can have just one husband. Men can have more than one wife only under certain conditions, however. The man must be able to support more than one wife financially and must treat all wives fairly and equally. Weddings take place in a mosque or in the bride's home, and traditionally the bride's hands and feet are decorated in intricate patterns with a dye called henna.

Another joyous occasion for Muslims is the birth of a baby. The child's father or another relative present at the time of the

A Muslim bride, her hands decorated with henna, signed her marriage certificate.

birth whispers prayers in the baby's ear. The baby's parents put a drop of honey on the baby's tongue, so his or her first taste is a sweet one. When the baby is about a week old, he or she is given a name.

Since the beginning of Islam, education has always been very important to Muslims. Children are encouraged to read the Qur'an and memorize it. Some then go to schools called *madrassas* and eventually to universities. Muslim education, while based on religion, has very high standards and has produced respected scientists, writers, artists, and doctors.

When a Muslim dies, his or her body is bathed and then wrapped in a plain cloth. Family and friends gather to say prayers for the dead person. In a simple grave, the body is buried facing the holy city of Mecca.

A Muslim cemetery in Fes, Morocco

Chapter Four

FROM MECCA TO
THE WORLD

It was in the important trading center of Mecca
that Islam began. The religion that worshipped
one God rose to greatness in a city where
people believed in many gods. But
Mecca was also home to
Christians and Jewish
traders, whose religions
honored one God.

*Mecca is a
modern city with
a population of
about 1.7 million.*

Muhammad, the founder of Islam, was born in Mecca in 570. His father died soon after he was born, and about six years later his mother died. The young orphan was raised by a grandfather and then an uncle. As he grew up, Muhammad did not learn to read or write. It is believed that he worked for a time as a shepherd.

When he was about 25, Muhammad began working for a rich female merchant named Khadijah. The young man proved to be intelligent and reliable, and eventually Khadijah asked Muhammad to marry her. After their marriage, Muhammad was rich, but he was still sympathetic to poor people and never was very happy as a member of the merchant class. By the time he was 40, Muhammad had begun meditating in the Cave of Hira. Muslims believe it was when Muhammad was meditating in the cave that he was visited by the angel Jibrail.

After going from Mecca to Medina in 622, Muhammad led the spread of Islam. He faced resistance from tribes in Medina, but the Muslims defeated them. He also encountered problems when

The angel Jibrail is known to Christians and Jews as Gabriel.

The Kaaba

In the center of Mecca is a large cube-shaped structure known as the Kaaba. For many years, the people of Mecca worshipped the Kaaba and the idols around it. On the Kabba is the Black Stone. Some people believe that the stone was given to Adam when he left the Garden of Eden. Other people believe it is a meteor. No matter what is true, the Kaaba is sacred to Muslims.

In 630 Muhammad laid his hands on the Kaaba and said, "Allahu Akbar." This was his way of affirming that there is but one God. He had the idols destroyed and stopped the worship of them. From that day on, the Kaaba was seen as a sacred sanctuary of Islam.

The Kaaba is more than 2,000 years old and has been repaired and rebuilt many times.

he tried to return to Mecca to visit the Kaaba. But the Meccans eventually allowed him back in the city. When Muhammad died in 632, there was suddenly a huge problem. Who would take his place and lead Islam?

In the end, Abu Bakr, who was a friend of Muhammad's, became the first *caliph* (leader) of Islam. But some people thought Muhammad's cousin Ali ibn Abi Talib should have been chosen. After Abu Bakr died in 634, he was followed by two other caliphs—Umar and Uthman ibn aAffan—and then by Ali ibn Abi Talib. When Ali came to power in 656 after Uthman was assassinated, a civil war began. It was basically a series of revolts against Ali.

The disagreements about Islamic leadership eventually led to a split among Muslims. One group, the Sunni, accepted Abu Bakr as the first caliph, and they believed that caliphs should be elected by Muslims.

Another group, the Shi'a, believed that Ali ibn Abi Talib was the only rightful caliph and that future caliphs should be related to him. This disagreement is such an obstacle to the Sunni and the Shi'a that it still has not been resolved after 1,300 years.

Located in western Saudi Arabia, Medina is said to be the city where Muhammad was buried.

Under the first four caliphs, known as the Rashidun, the Islamic religion became powerful in the Middle East, spreading from the Arabian Peninsula to Spain. As the faith became more prominent, some Muslims began to question the direction it was taking. They were not interested in wealth and power. Their goals were spiritual. This group became the Sufis.

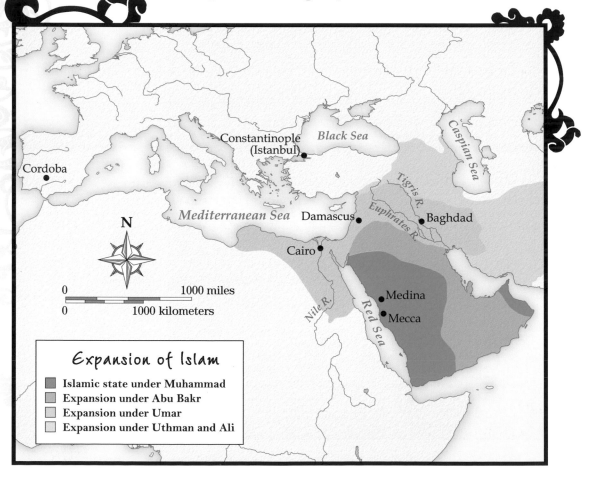

Cordoba

Constantinople (Istanbul)

Black Sea

Caspian Sea

Mediterranean Sea   Damascus

Tigris R.

Euphrates R.

Baghdad

Cairo

Nile R.

Red Sea

Medina

Mecca

N

0   1000 miles

0   1000 kilometers

Expansion of Islam

◼ Islamic state under Muhammad
◼ Expansion under Abu Bakr
◼ Expansion under Umar
◼ Expansion under Uthman and Ali

Following the Rashidun, the Muslim world was divided into caliphates. These included the Umayyads (whose capital was Damascus, Syria, and then Cordoba, Spain), the Abbasids (in Baghdad, Iraq), the Fatimids (in Cairo, Egypt), and the Ottomans (in Istanbul, Turkey).

From 750 to 1258, Islam experienced what is known as its Golden Age. Muslim scientists, artists, writers, business leaders, philosophers, and others made significant contributions to the world. As the religion grew, Muslim regions began trading with other nations. As more people began doing business with one another, more inventions and innovations were created.

For example, Muslim farmers introduced a crop rotation system that let them grow various crops on the same land. They also developed efficient watering practices. Muslim scientist Ibn al-Haytham made great strides in the field of optics, and he invented the camera obscura, a device that eventually led to photography.

Muslim doctors created some of the world's first medical schools and hospitals. One physician, Abu al-Qasim, invented several surgical tools, including the scalpel. Other doctors made discoveries about diseases and how the body's circulation system worked.

Muslim architecture flourished during the Golden Age. The Great Mosque of Xi'an in China and the Great

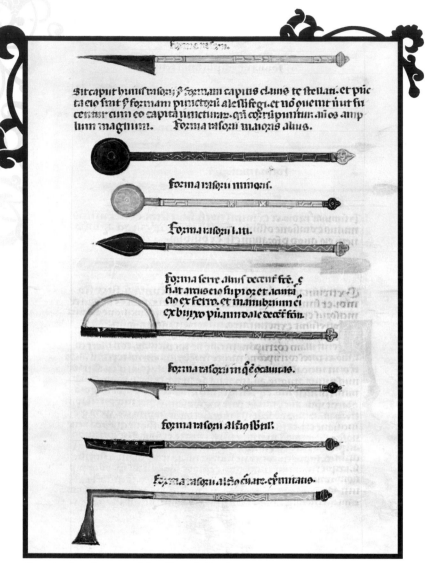

Surgical tools created by Abu al-Qasim

Mosque in Cordoba were built during this time. Muslim artists developed calligraphy, a system of writing that was used for architecture and Arabic writing. "Allah is beautiful and loves beauty" is an Islamic saying.

The Muslim mosque in Xi'an is one of the biggest and best-preserved of the early mosques in China.

This beauty can be seen in Islamic textiles, paintings, and ceramics.

But Islam faced many challenges during the Golden Age. Among them were the Crusades, the Reconquista, and the Mongol invasion.

The Crusades were a series of military attacks by

Christian Western Europeans from 1025 to the 1200s. The Crusaders were trying to regain control of the Holy Land from the Muslims. But they were fiercely resisted by Saladin, a Muslim general who took control of Jerusalem in 1187. By 1193 most of the areas seized by the Crusaders had been returned to Islamic control.

The Reconquista was a series of efforts by Christian kingdoms to expel Muslims from the Iberian Peninsula,

Saladin, the leader of the Islamic forces during the third crusade, is honored as a hero. He recaptured the city of Jerusalem from the Christians in the 12th century.

which includes present-day Spain and Portugal. The Reconquista ended in 1492, when Muslim ruler Muhammad XII surrendered his kingdom to Christian monarchs King Ferdinand and Queen Isabella.

In the 1200s, forces from the Mongol Empire invaded many Islamic lands. At the height of its power, the Mongol Empire stretched from Eastern Europe across Asia, creating the largest connected empire in the history of the world. The Mongols' invasion of Baghdad in 1258 nearly destroyed the city. For a time, Islam was

Mongols under the leadership of Hulagu Khan captured Baghdad in 1258.

replaced by Buddhism as the dominant religion in Asia. But over the next century, some Mongol leaders converted to Islam, and the religion began to grow once again.

Rumi

Mawlana Jalal Muhammad Balkhi (1207–1273) was a poet and religious thinker best known to English speakers by the name Rumi. He was born in present-day Afghanistan, which was then part of the Persian Empire. He and his family fled that region during the Mongol invasion and traveled through many Muslim lands and made a pilgrimage to Mecca. He eventually settled in Konya, now part of Turkey. His parents were both religious scholars, and at a young age Rumi himself became a religious teacher. He was introduced to mysticism by a dervish, an Islamic holy man, named Shamsuddin of Tabriz. After Shamsuddin's death, Rumi began writing music and poetry. One of his best-known works is the *Masnavi*, a text that to Sufis is almost as important as the Qur'an.

Despite losses such as those during the Reconquista, the Muslim world expanded as more people adopted Islam. In the 1500s, Shi'a Islam became the official religion of Persia (now known as Iran). Islam also grew in Turkey, especially when the Ottoman Empire flourished, reaching its height in 1672. In the early 1900s, there was a huge shift. The Ottoman Empire ended after World War I (1914–1918), and the old system of Muslim caliphate leadership ended in 1924.

In the 20th century, Islam underwent many changes. Muslims have moved to many parts of the world, starting communities in the Caribbean and in North and South America. The Organization of the Islamic Conference was created in 1969 to promote and protect Islamic values. Its members are in 57 nations, and it is represented at the United Nations. In 1990 the OIC issued the Cairo Declaration on Human Rights in Islam, which summarizes Islamic ideals.

Chapter Five

ISLAM TODAY

Islam today is the religion of nearly one-fourth of the people in the world. Only Christianity has more followers. In almost 40 countries, Islam is the main religion. The countries with the greatest Muslim populations are India, Pakistan, Indonesia, and Bangladesh.

Most Muslims live in Asia and Africa, but there are also significant populations in Europe, North America, and South America. Many people think Islam is just dominant in the Arab countries of the Middle East, but only about 20 percent of Muslims are Arab people. Today you can meet a person with Islamic beliefs almost anywhere in the world.

Islamic practices vary from country to country, but in many places the religion plays a big role in government. In Saudi Arabia, for example, almost every citizen is a Muslim. Its leader, King Abdullah, rules his people according to Islamic law. In some Islamic countries, people are not allowed to vote, and strict rules control what clothing women can wear and how they live. In other places, such as in Europe and North America, all Muslims have the rights other citizens have.

Over the years, there has been much conflict between Muslim nations and Western nations. One conflict involves the division of Palestine, which occurred in 1947. The United Nations decided to divide the territory to create a homeland for Jews displaced after World War II. Part of Palestine was given to the Jewish people and part

King Abdullah, who has ruled Saudi Arabia since 2005, has called for talks among Muslim, Christian, and Jewish leaders.

Islamic Law

The major rules of Islamic law are based on the teachings of the Qur'an and on the Sunnah, which are the traditions and practices of Muhammad. The laws guide the lives of Muslims. One, for example, is about fasting. If a Muslim forgets and has a bite of food during a fast, the fast is still acceptable. But if the person eats on purpose, the fast is no longer valid. The laws may also control how men and women interact and when a divorce is allowed. Sometimes the meanings of the laws are not clear. Interpreting the laws depends partly upon *ijma*, which is the agreement of Muslim scholars. It also depends on *qiyas*, which is a new rule based on thought and reasoning. Sometimes a disagreement about the laws leads to a *fatwa*, a ruling by an Islamic religious leader.

of it to the Muslim people who lived there. The Jewish people named their section Israel and expelled Muslims who had lived there for generations. Many Muslims were angry because Jewish people had control over land they

felt was rightfully theirs. But many Western nations backed Israel then and continue to do so today. This is one reason many Muslims do not trust Western nations. They worry that people in the West will try to change Muslims' religion and their way of life.

Pakistani protesters marched during an anti-Israel protest in Lahore in January 2009.

Images of Muhammad

Islamic tradition bans the use of images of Muhammad. So in 2005, when a Danish newspaper published cartoons using Muhammad's image, Muslims were outraged. Protests erupted throughout the Muslim world, and some of these protests became violent. Officials from the newspaper eventually apologized for printing the cartoons but held firm to the belief that under Danish law they had the right to print them.

Over the years, some people in Western nations have begun to fear Muslims. Some Muslims have carried out violent acts in the name of their religion. They are religious extremists—people who take the beliefs of a religion to the extreme. They may even kill people who disagree with their beliefs. Some Islamic extremists belong to groups called the Taliban and al-Qaeda. Their members have committed crimes, such as hijacking planes and killing national leaders and other people. Most people believe that Islamic extremists were to blame for the September 11, 2001, attacks on the World Trade Center in New York City and the Pentagon in Washington, D.C., that killed thousands.

Because of the actions of the extremists, some Muslims in the United States and other countries have been mistreated. People sometimes think all followers

Muslims gathered in prayer at the Islamic Center of America in Dearborn, Michigan, to celebrate Eid al-Fitr, which marked the end of Ramadan.

of Islam have extremist beliefs. But most Muslims are not extremists. Like people all over the world, most Muslims respect other religions, love their families, and believe in peace.

Mustafa Ceric (left), a Bosnian Muslim leader, and Pope Benedict XVI met at the Vatican, the pope's home in Italy, to talk about the importance of religious freedom and peace.

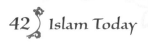

In November 2008, Islamic and Roman Catholic leaders took a big step forward in understanding one another. They discussed the concerns both groups had about the world. They talked about terrorism, poverty,

and religious tolerance. Pope Benedict XVI said, "Let us resolve to overcome past prejudices and to correct the often distorted images of the other, which even today can create difficulties in our relations." The conference was an important opportunity for people of all religions to understand and appreciate the history and ideals of Islam.

TIMELINE

570   Muhammad is born in Mecca

610   The angel Jibrail is said to have visited Muhammad

622   Mohammad founds Islam

632   Muhammad dies

750   Islam's Golden Age begins

1187   Saladin defeats the Crusaders and takes Jerusalem

1258   The Mongol army invades Baghdad

1672   The Ottoman Empire reaches its height

1924   The caliphate system ends

1947   Palestine is divided, leading to the creation of Israel in 1948

1969   The Organization of the Islamic Conference is created

1990   The OIC issues the Cairo Declaration of Human Rights in Islam

2001   The United States is attacked on September 11; most people believe members of al-Qaeda are responsible

2008   In November Catholic and Muslim leaders meet to condemn terrorism, fight poverty throughout the world, and encourage religious tolerance

Muslims use only their right hands for eating, and they enter mosques with their right feet first.

The first algebra book was published by a Muslim mathematician in the 11th century. The word *algebra* comes from the Islamic *al jabr,* which means "completion."

The largest mosque in the world is the Shah Fiesal in Islamabad, Pakistan. It can hold 100,000 people.

Al-Azhar University in Cairo was founded in 975 and is the world center of Arabic literature and Sunni Islamic education.

Along with prayer, almsgiving is another duty of Muslims. The Qur'an says it is important to give to the needy. Many Muslims pay special taxes that are used to help the poor, orphans, and others in need.

Muslims believe that on the last day, the world will be destroyed, and Allah will raise all people from the dead to be judged. People who were good in life will go to Paradise, while those who were bad will go to Hell. However, people who have died know before the last day whether they will go to Paradise or to Hell. Muslims believe that those headed for Hell suffer in their graves, while those bound for Paradise rest in peace until the last day.

GLOSSARY

assassinated—murdered an important person by secret and sudden attack

caliph—leader of Islam

deity—god or goddess

dervish—Islamic holy man who belongs to a religious order known for its devotional exercises, such as bodily movements that lead to a trance

halal—foods that have been blessed so Muslims can eat them

Holy Land—region in the Middle East that includes Jerusalem and is of religious significance to Muslims, Jews, and Christians

idols—objects of worship

imam—person who leads prayers in a mosque

jihad—religious duty to follow the way of Allah; can sometimes lead to holy war

madrassas—Muslim religious schools

meditate—concentrate on emptying the mind of thought

Middle East—region that includes countries in western Asia and parts of North Africa

minaret—tower in a mosque from which Muslims are called to prayer

mosque—Muslim place of worship

muezzin—person who calls Muslims to prayer

mysticism—belief that direct knowledge of God can be found through individual experience

pagan—someone who doesn't belong to any major world religion

pilgrimage—journey to a religious place

prophet—person who hears God and shares messages from him

Qur'an—sacred book of Islam

Sunnah—traditions and practices of Muhammad

Western—relating to countries such as the United States, Canada, and those in western Europe

FURTHER REFERENCE

Nonfiction

Heiligman, Deborah. *Celebrate Ramadan & Eid al-Fitr.*
Washington, D.C.: National Geographic Society, 2006.

Wallace, Holly. *This Is My Faith: Islam.* Hauppage, N.Y.:
Barron's Educational Publishing, 2006.

Wilkinson, Philip. *Eyewitness Islam.* New York: DK
Publishing, 2002.

Fiction

Abdel-Fattah, Randa. *Does My Head Look Big in This?* New
York: Orchard Books, 2007.

Khan, Rukhsana. *Muslim Child: A Collection of Short Stories and
Poems.* Toronto: Napoleon Publishing, 1999.

Nye, Naomi Shihab. *Habibi.* New York: Simon & Schuster
Books for Young Readers, 1997.

Internet Sites

FactHound offers a safe, fun way to find Internet sites
related to this book. All of the sites on FactHound have
been researched by our staff.

Here's all you do:

Visit *www.facthound.com*

FactHound will fetch the best sites for you!

INDEX

ABOUT THE AUTHOR

Lucia Raatma has written dozens of books for young readers. They are about famous people, historical events, ways to stay safe, and other topics. She lives in Florida's Tampa Bay area with her husband and their two children.

FEB   2010